Lucid Dreaming

Lucid dreams: A Beginner's Guide On How To Control Your Dreams With Different Techniques.

Austin Knight

JAN   2017

Table of Contents

Introduction

As life is full of new and exciting experiences, so are dreams. Dreams in general are defined as images, sensations and thoughts that occur while one sleeps. Everyone dreams, but most of the time we are unable to recall what happened.

The Key to lucid dreaming is defined with the use of two main types of lucid dreams. The first is Wake Induced Lucid Dreaming (WILD) and the second is Dream Induced Lucid Dreaming (DILD). WILD is handing over your awareness from a physically woken state directly to a sleeping lucid dream state.

Where as DILD dreams happen more frequently than WILDs. A study of 76 lucid dreamers showed only one-quarter of them were wake initiated. The man who'd completed the study, Dr. Stephen LaBerge, believed even those numbers were skewed. It's his belief that WILDs occur more frequently in a lab setting than they do at home.

As we go through life we would spend several waking hours questioning dreams, why we have them and how can we control them? What is lucid dreaming? How do you remember a dream? How do you know that you are dreaming? How can you control your dreams with lucidity? Theses may be questions you are asking yourself... well there is a simple answer to all of these questions. Read on into the depths of this book and not only will you find yourself learning in great detail about lucid dreaming but you will learn techniques to control your dreams.

Imagine the potential you can have with having the control over your dream state rather than being a spectator in your dreams. Some people say that they cannot remember their dreams or they simply do not dream. But those people are misled and you will be satisfied with the answers within this informative novella. This novella will provide evidence to you that everyone is capable of having a lucid dream, it only comes down to the will power you have in order to achieve your goal.

Lucid Dreams are the most enjoyable thing to do with your subconscious, you have the potential to soar high into the sky with your spectacular white angel wings and forget about reality. Or You can flip the switch and turn a night mare into a dream of your control. Instead of being terrorized by Clowns you will have the skills to terrorize them.

Chapter 1 – Eleven Signs You're a Lucid Dreamer

Some people are actually born lucid dreamers. I've met such a man and I love hearing his stories about how he's always been able to control his dreams, ever since he was a child. Others, like us, have to work at becoming a lucid dreamer. Regardless of which end of the spectrum you fall under, here are eleven signs that you are ready to take control of those dreams and make them lucid.

1. You have intense daydreams. Intense means vivid, wild and you find it easy to slip into those daydreams. You are also able to fantasize easily and with great detail.

2. You are able to wake naturally several days per week, without an alarm.

3. You can recall your dreams easily most nights. This is crucial to lucid dreaming. The ability to have strong recall will also make your dreams more vivid.

4. Your dreams are often intense.

5. You've had lucid dreams in the past.

6. You've been able to wake yourself up from a nightmare in the past.

7. You meditate several times per week, if not every day.

8. You keep a dream journal and discuss your dreams regularly. This can be a discussion you have with yourself. Obviously if you are uncomfortable sharing the content of your dreams with your coworkers, that is unnecessary. Keeping the dream journal is great for the discussion part because you can simply read it aloud to yourself.

9. You play a lot of first person video games. Years of research has shown that spending your waking time with stimulated realities provided by video games has a huge impact on your dreams at night.

10. You experience out of body sensations or sleep paralysis. Scary as those may sound, they are actually the beginning of an intensely lucid dream. It is less common, but a lucid dream all the same.

11. You have a strong desire to control your dreams. Saying you intend to have a lucid dream aloud is sometimes all it takes to get into that state. Dreams are comprised of your thoughts and intentions. Setting that before you fall asleep increases the likelihood of a lucid dream.

You may have experienced all or even just one of these. You don't need to have checked off every item on this list to get to lucid dreaming. Along with practice and meditation, you'll find yourself lucid dreaming in no time.

Chapter 2 – Dreams Defined

Dreams in general are defined as images, sensations and thoughts that occur while one sleeps. Everyone dreams, but most of the time we are unable to recall what happened. That first moment when you wake up from a great dream, all of the details are so vivid. Aromas and feelings are right there at your fingertips. Then, in the blink of an eye, it is gone. On occasion, we can remember one or two details of a dream.

There is a difference between a typical dream and that of lucid dreaming. The ability to have a lucid dream is defined as a person consciously being able to observe or control a dream. Not only can one recall the colors, feelings, touch and smell, they actually were able to control all of those elements and bring them together. With a normal dream, we have no control. Sometimes there is chaos, horror, joy, and even wet dreams. Lucid dreaming means you are in control of what happens. In its simplest of terms, lucid dreaming is being aware of the fact a dream is taking place while in the REM cycle of sleep, which is where all dreams occur. (Rapid eye movement whilst sleeping and the paralysis of the muscle)

Many times, after we've woken from a particularly wonderful dream we wonder why we aren't able to hold onto those memories. What's great about lucid dreaming is those memories and everything that happened in your dream can be something you remember vividly. It's an entirely new world ready to explore. In dreams, the five senses are lost because sleep is an unconscious state. Imagine what it would be like to know those senses in your dream. Touch, smell, sight, hearing and even taste can be experienced through lucid dreaming.

Lucid dreaming isn't something people can lay down, fall asleep and leap right into. It is a process that takes time to understand, develop and implement properly. There are no downsides to lucid dreaming. If you do something "wrong" the world will not implode and no magical doorway unleashing indestructible beasts will open. It's your world. Your senses. Your journey. It's a place where you can find treasure, sing opera, write best-selling novels or sleep with your favorite actor/actress. When you are in a world where there are no limits, the possibilities are endless.

It might help to think about your body as being a glove. While you are awake, you are confined to the limitations of that body. You can't fly outside of a plane and you can't explore space without being an astronaut. Our bodies are what keep us grounded and there is absolutely nothing wrong with that. It's part of being human and being alive, both of which are wonderful things. Lucid dreaming is our chance to do things we never thought possible. In the world of dreams, we are no longer restricted. The glove comes off and we are free to do whatever we desire.

Ultimately, there a millions of possibilities. While you sleep, you are connected to the wondrous thing that is *yourself*. You have unbounded potential. Being lucid while you sleep enables you to begin to explore the things you want to become. You build the life you wanted to create for yourself and eventually, you are able to channel those extraordinary possibilities and bring them to your waking life.

Chapter 3 – Benefits of Lucid Dreaming

There are several benefits of lucid dreaming. We briefly touched on how it can bring your dreams to life in the sense that you are exploring all of your potential. Some of the benefits include the ability to promote physical and psychological healing, helping to solve problems in your daily life, practicing actual life skills, discovering deep history about yourself, finding and unfolding your emotional and even sexual self. You are learning to explore the universe that resides inside you.

Promoting physical and psychological healing is important to us as humans. During our waking life, we want our bodies to be strong, healthy and able. Under normal circumstances, the body is able to function quite well without any help from us. Internally, it is always working to fight off disease and fatigue without too much strain on your mind, or impacting your daily life. What about old habits, or even mild psychological issues, though. Interestingly enough, ancient Greeks and Romans built hundreds of healing temples to deal with these types of issues. Today, most of those are dealt with through counseling or even drugs when something as wonderful as lucid dreaming could work wonders. The imagery in your dreams is the way we are able to communicate with unconscious body processes...like bad habits or mild mental issues. Once you are able to get a firm grasp on lucid dreaming, you can work toward your own self-healing. Lucid dreaming offers the chance for you to enter yourself and reprogram the hardwiring, which is a wonderful way of self-help.

Lucid dreaming can also help solve problems in your daily life. We are all capable of problem-solving on some level. There are people who are better at it than others. Throughout your entire life, you've learned incredible things all on your own. Reading, writing, building your vocabulary...all of those things you've amassed simply by living in a civilized society. All this time, you've also been absorbing things in the world around you subconsciously. You've taken in millions of pieces of information and stored them in your mind without actually making a conscious effort. Things you've acknowledged as intuition or a gut instinct were because of what you learned in life, not what was taught in a classroom.

Dreams can take you beyond what you know and the things you are comfortable with. Problem-solving while awake is limiting in that it deals largely with things you have either previously dealt with, or have read about, perhaps seen on television. In dreams, there are oceans of experience waiting to be explored. Lucidity is what allows the creativeness to transform imagery into insight, and that is where creative problem-solving begins.

Some time ago, a researcher discovered that cats that had damaged a certain part of their brain lived out their dreams with movement. They would crouch and jump at imaginary prey and the researcher deduced that this is one of the ways dreaming can help to practice life skills. With damaged brains, the cats wouldn't be able to survive in the outside world, but they were able to practice the things cats are known for through dreaming and imagination.

In that respect, lucidity can help enhance that possibility. Dreams are a place you can live without the risk of getting hurt, either physically or emotionally. In dreams, you are able to explore different relationships, new skills, life situations, creativity or even sexuality because dreams provide that world of limitless possibility. The world you create is entirely up to you. In dreams, you are entirely in control, imagine the possibility's in what you can do with your sexual fantasies.

With lucid dreaming, you can also find your true potential. As a human, we ask questions and seek answers to find what we are truly capable of. We are lead to believe that people who are exceptionally talented must have been born with that gift and that we could never achieve what they have. Perhaps they had a more advantageous start in life, but that does not mean that we are incapable of achieving great things. Every night when you dream, you are the creator. You make unique situations that are creative only to you. That means there is creativity alive deep within and lucidity can help bring that to your waking life.

Lucidity can help you discover your deepest roots... Your dreams can give you something most people never find and that is a deep connection and memory beyond your years. Everything around you are connected. They may have an independent existence, but they are all still connected. Perhaps lucid dreaming will help you discover a past life or a memory from when you were very young. Most research shows people are not able to remember what happened to them as a very young child. Lucid dreaming could make that a possibility.

Another great thing lucidity can help you discover is your true emotional self. Perhaps you feel stuck...like you've achieved all you can in life. This could be because your creative, emotional and mental energy has halted or maybe it was never fully given the opportunity to develop. There is always room for improvement, always the possibility to grow. There is also more love, self-worth, self-compassion and even sexual satisfaction to be found.

Lucidity can help you discover the universe that resides within you. World renowned psychiatrist Carl Jung once described the subconscious as something that should never be ignored. He went on to say that it is as limitless, as natural and even as powerful as the stars themselves. Over several years another doctor by the name of Stanislav Grof studied people's claims that they could remember being an infant, time in the womb and describing things that would have happened in a different life. Some even went on to detail ancient Egyptian mummification rituals. Dr. Grof concluded that what we all know as reality is superficial. He went on to say that our lives as humans are incorrect and incomplete. We learn our limitations throughout life. Lucid dreaming is a way to unlearn those limitations and discover the universe within yourself.

Chapter 4 – Total (Dream) Recall

There are several elements to dream lucidity and one of the first things to try to do is recalling your dreams. This is where journaling will come in handy. Keep one next to your bed so that the first thing you do when you wake from a dream is to write down every detail you recall. The longer you are awake after a dream, the less you will be able to remember. They fade rather quickly, so it's best to take this step as soon as you possibly can.

Over the course of the night and our whopping one-hundred minutes of dream time, we have several different dreams. Sometimes they are all part of the same theme, others its complete chaos and there is no fluidity from one dream to the next. What you'll want to remember is that in order to lucid dream, you'll want to practice recalling at least one vivid dream per night. This step helps to boost self-awareness and helps to you actually remember your lucid dreams when they happen. Self-awareness is what makes lucidity more likely.

Below, we will detail four tips on how to remember your dreams on a regular basis. The more frequent, the better. Even if you think you don't dream because you never remember them, you do. Only a small percentage of people who suffer from a very rare sleep disorder do not have dreams.

Step one is to sleep well. It might sound as though we are stating the obvious, but it is incredibly important. During the first four to six hours of sleep, your brain prioritizes NREM (Non-Rapid Eye Movement). This is where the body can get its much needed rest and physically repair itself. During this time, you will dream, but in short bursts. There isn't much to recall and it is hard to get a grasp on what exactly is going on.

After you've gone through NREM, you'll pass into REM sleep, which is where your mind will unload emotions and psychologically repair itself. During REM you'll find the greatest potential for lucid dreaming. Basically, if you are unable to get a decent amount of sleep on a regular basis, you'll find it difficult to obtain lucid dreams because you are experiencing less dreams overall. Not only will you be unlikely to obtain lucid dreams, lack of sleep is bad for your overall mental and physical health. Work on getting the recommended eight hours. You'll feel good and you'll be able to lucid dream.

The next step, as we mentioned earlier, is keeping a dream journal. Once you've gotten your body to a point that its getting tons of REM sleep, you will want to actively record all of the dreams you recall. Even if you aren't the most talented artist in the world (admittedly, my best artwork is stick figures) try to keep both an illustrated and written journal. Sometimes it is difficult to put something you've seen or experienced into words. Draw it up!

Take the first five to ten minutes after you've woken to write or draw in your dream journal. Write down all of the details you remember. It doesn't have to be neat or even in full sentences. The quicker you get the details down, the better. Make sure to take special note of unusual symbols, scenes, emotions or people by underlining them. Also, a good tip here is to write in present tense. Yes, the dream already happened and is technically past tense, but it helps lucidity to write as though they are happening.

Before we move onto the next step, I'd like to mention a dream recall experiment. It involves some serious commitment, but is undoubtedly worth the effort. What you'll need to do sounds crazy. Wake yourself at the end of your sleep cycles to coincide with your REM sleep. Studies show that we recall things with much more clarity when waking directly from a dream.

The free way to do this is to set your smartphone to wake you about 4.5 to 5 hours after you've gone to sleep. With some luck, you'll wake up right after the first big chunk of REM sleep. Write down everything you remember immediately upon waking.

For the rest of the night, have your alarm go off at ninety minute intervals. If it takes you longer than normal to get to sleep, you'll want to extend that by about ten to twenty minutes, depending on how long it takes for you to achieve sleep once your head hits the pillow. It's probably best to try this on a weekend night when you know you don't have anything important to do the next day. It's possible you'll be tired from all of the interrupted sleep. However, it is still a great experiment to try at least once while trying to obtain lucidity.

The second method is to use a Fitbit. What's great about this product is it is relatively inexpensive (if you get the Flex or the One) and when connected to your smartphone, it records your sleep patterns. Additionally, you can set a silent alarm that won't wake your partner, cat, dog, or kids several times during the night while you are experimenting. There is another, newly released way to track your sleep called the Neuroon sleep mask. It is incredibly technological and can track your brainwaves, much like an EEG. It uses sound and light to let you know that you are dreaming, which is really neat! It's intention is to help bring awareness to the fact that you are dreaming. The Neuroon is about three-hundred dollars whereas you can purchase the Fitbit One for ninety-nine and the Flex for about one-hundred and twenty.

The goal of the sleep experiment is to recall at least five, vivid dreams. At the end of this experiment, you will probably be surprised to see just how much you do dream and how many dreams you experience each night. It's important to note that this isn't the type of experiment you want to try several nights in a row or on a regular basis. Waking yourself that much during the night regularly is bad for your overall health.

Moving on to step three in dream recall is the use of a B6 supplement. A double-blind study conducted in 2002 showed that people who took 250mg of B6 daily experienced increased dream content. This included vividness, increase in emotions, more vibrant colors and even bizarreness. You can obtain this with as little as 100mg per day. Start low and work your way up to find the right dose for you. As always, check with your medical professional to make sure that taking this supplement won't interfere with any medications or supplements you may already be taking. We don't want to do anything counterintuitive to your health.

Those are the main steps in dream recall. They can be done in any order, or you may find that only one or two works for you. Ultimately, the use of a vitamin or supplement is at your own discretion. No matter what, the best thing you can do to increase your chances of lucidity is to keep a dream journal.

Chapter 5 – Dream Signs

There are four types of dream signs that will aid you in becoming lucid. You'll want to learn to recognize these dream signs and use them to trigger that conscious lucidity while dreaming. Dr. LaBerge created a dream sign inventory for us to use as a way of achieving our lucid dreaming goal. Most lucid dreamers use dream signs to help them recognize when they are dreaming. These signs give you the clues necessary to find lucidity. They also help your rational brain to make that all-important realization that a dream is taking place.

What are dream signs, you ask? They can be a plethora of things from a deceased loved one, talking animals or fruit, an oddly shaped door or even something as small as the handle on the door being out of place or misshapen. The point is, there are millions of dream signs and what you need to do is recognize those that are specific to you and your dreams.

Most of the time, dream signs will be significant to you and they are what will cue you in to the fact that you are dreaming. Something will be out of place, moved from where you always keep it. Perhaps a window is missing, or the door is on the ceiling. It will be something you know to be odd.

First, inner awareness. This is where you will realize there is something unusual about the dream in the way of thoughts, emotions, perception or sensation. An example of this is thinking about yourself lifting off the ground and then actually being able to do it.

The next dream sign is action. There are some physical activities that are just plain wrong. This can be you personally or people in your dream, even inanimate objects. An example of this can be people moving backward while you move forward, perhaps there is a dog flying on its leash while the owner walks it. Anything incredibly unusual in the way of action.

The third dream sign is that of form. Usually this has to do with how a person looks. Their body will be an abnormal shape or unusual height, perhaps their arms are so long they drag on the ground behind them as they move. Shrunken heads are a common theme when it comes to form.

The last dream sign is that of context. This has to do with the situation you find yourself in while dreaming. If it is something that is impossible or contrary to your real life, it is a dream sign. Also, anything that might be contradictory to you in your waking life. Perhaps you are drinking a glass of scotch, but you've never drank before, or in your dream you are male while awake you are female. The context in a dream is obvious once you get to be familiar with the sign.

We've also touched on waking activities that will help with lucidity and there are two that you can work on that will help you with recognizing dream signs. The steps are simple and will help you cue yourself in to those dream signs.

First, the reality check. While you are awake, your goal on a daily basis is to recognize when things seem out of place. You can practice using the reality check while sitting on your couch watching the sci-fi channel or supernatural movies or television shows. Obviously, they will have several elements of things being out of place. Question all of them and their nature. It's a simple trick that will help you in your dreams.

Cataloguing your dream signs is the second trick. Your aforementioned dream journal will be where you keep this catalogue. Underline every dream sign and to go a little deeper here, categorize them into subgroups that will correspond with the steps Dr. LaBerge outlined for us and were discussed previously in this chapter. They are; inner awareness, context, form and action. Record several dreams using this technique, then look for recurring signs and the most common type of dream you are experiencing. This will help you identify your dream signs during the lucid dream. No matter which of the dream signs is most common to you, look for potential differences in your waking life and you will discover that they will be far more noticeable in dreams.

Chapter 6 – The Five Types of Dreams

The first of the five is known as daydreaming. During this state of mind, you are awake, but not checked in to what's going on around you. Daydreaming is quite common and studies have shown that people will daydream from 70 to 120 minutes per day, while they are awake. In a daydream, you enter a hypnotic state of mind, which allows unconscious thoughts, memories and ideas to come to life. Daydreams start with a compelling thought or memory, and your imagination takes over from there. Some research has shown that people who daydream more often are able to find lucidity in dreams while they sleep easier than those that don't. This is in large part due to the fact that daydreaming is practicing lucid dreaming. Daydreams are really great. They are a healthy way to temporarily escape the mundane, release frustration, or get away from a harsh reality.

The second type is a normal dream. The normal dream makes an appearance during a person's REM cycle of sleep. In general, if you achieve eight hours of sleep per night, 100 minutes of that will be spent dreaming. The more vivid and longer dreams tend to occur right before you wake up. Dreams are wonderful in that a lot of times you have no idea you are dreaming until you wake. Your subconscious makes it so you accept your dream reality and take it for what it is in that moment.

Next is the lucid dream, the main focus of this book and they really are the best type of dream to have. There is no greater feeling of freedom or unlimited possibilities than what happens during a lucid dream. You are in control and can guide your dream in any direction you choose. There are two things that define a lucid dream. The first is knowing that you are in a dream and the second is the ability to control the dream or direct your awareness. Lucid dreams provide brilliant insight into your unconscious mind.

The fourth type of dream is called a false awakening. This is exactly what it implies. You wake up, go through your normal morning routine only to find you've not actually woken up. You may get as far as turning into your office building before you realize you are still dreaming and *then* you wake up. False awakenings are quite vivid dreams. It seems as though your brain is functioning by getting you up out of bed and going through all the motion you normally would. Even the most minute details of the room are there. The alarm clock changes time, the sun is peaking through the shades and you can feel your body moving. These types of dreams usually end with some kind of shocking revelation. It can be your looking in the mirror to see you've regressed to your teenage self or as you drive to work you see there are absolutely no other cars on the road. Eventually, you wake up and realize that you were still dreaming.

Finally, the fifth and most dreaded type of dream is that of nightmares. We all have them and as much as we try to avoid them, there is little that can be done. Nightmares should be rare occurrences and they are usually caused by stress or trauma, drugs or alcohol, some sicknesses and on occasion, watching a horror movie can trigger a nightmare. The last isn't something that is scientifically proven and is just a theory. Nightmares are generally vivid, just like the false awakening. Sometimes, they can be so vivid that it triggers your sensory system and you can feel emotion or even certain types of pain. Nightmares are undeniably the most unnerving of all the dreams. However, it is possible to turn a nightmare into a lucid dream, which means you can take over control of what's happening. Being able to take control of a nightmare is just one of the many benefits of lucid dreaming.

Chapter 7 – Let's Get WILD

There are two types of lucid dreams. The first is Wake Induced Lucid Dreaming (WILD) and the second is Dream Induced Lucid Dreaming (DILD). Moving forward, we will be referring to each by their acronym.

WILD is handing over your awareness from a physically woken state directly to a sleeping lucid dream state. Of the two, this is not the easiest technique, but it has two very big advantages. First, you basically have lucid dreaming on demand meaning you choose *when* to go lucid. The second is peak lucidity, which is the most vivid dream possible.

WILD stems from Tibetan Dream Yoga. It is a Buddhist philosophy used to find the path to enlightenment. This path is easiest when you meditate frequently, which will be detailed a little later on. WILD almost always requires extensive practice, though there are known cases in which children taught themselves this technique and have used it through adulthood. It is also known as "dreaming yourself to sleep." The key to this type of lucid dreaming is to know and understand your specific sleep signals. Once you are able to identify your sleep triggers, you will be able to use this process with ease.

We will briefly outline the process of WILD dreaming and provide step by step actions to take in order to achieve it. Remember that this isn't something that will come easily, so if you are unable to obtain WILD on your first try, don't worry! It's all about the experience and even a failed attempt at WILD is practice.

The first step is to get into the corpse pose. If you've ever studied yoga, it is also known as shavasana. Lie on your back with your body completely relaxed. Your legs are spread about hips width distance apart and your arms will be about six inches from your body with the palms facing up. Your body needs to be incredibly loose and the best time to achieve one is after about four to six hours of deep, restful sleep. Clear your mind. If any stray thoughts pop in, acknowledge them and send them on their way. Once all thoughts have passed, breathe slowly and deeply. Breathe in to the count of four, hold for seven seconds, then exhale for an eight count. After you've done that ten times, you should be completely relaxed. On a side note, this is actually great meditative practice for any time you are stressed.

Step two is getting into the state of hypnagogia. This is the transitional state between being awake and asleep. As you sink deeper into hypnagogia, there will be stages where you'll experience bright colors behind your eyelids. The second usually involves some kind of sound, though it shouldn't be startling. Distant music or voices are the most common. During this time, you will want to hold onto your conscious awareness. In order to have a WILD, you'll need to have that when you slip into a sleeping state.

Step three is to create a dream scene. When you get to a point where you can feel the dream state coming, you are ready to proceed. If you aren't feeling intense, fleeting memories, you aren't quite ready to proceed and can enjoy hypnogogia a little while longer. You will probably need to practice even getting to this point a few times before you are ready to proceed and that is just fine. Once you are able to get there, you'll realize it was totally worth it. If you have made it to this point and are ready to launch, go for it.

There are two ways to launch, which we'll discuss briefly now. The first method is known as visualization. Here is where you will be able to begin to visualize your dream in your mind's eye. Build on the landscape or the face of a dream character. Make it as vivid as you can. As the scene becomes more intense, place yourself in the middle of it and start to explore your surroundings calmly and peacefully.

The second method to launching is the out of body exit. This is the alternative route to WILD. On occasion, your body is so relaxed and you get so wrapped up in the hypnogogic state that you fall asleep. Don't beat yourself up if you do, that's what the out of body exit is for. When this occurs, there is nowhere else to go except your own bedroom. That's perfect because you are lucid dreaming. When you come to the realization that you are in your own room, you'll be able to launch out of your body. Because sometimes it may feel as though your body is paralyzed, physically getting up may not be possible. No need to panic. You can sink, float or swing yourself out of the paralysis. That is what happens in the out of body exit. In this state, expectation drives everything. Expect that you will be able to launch out of your body and it will happen. Again, it may take a lot of practice, but this is the kind of practice that is actually a lot of fun and you'll find you enjoy getting yourself into the lucid dreaming state.

Chapter 8 – DILD...Easy Lucidity

Dream induced lucid dreaming is much more common and quite frankly, easier to get into. In this state, lucid dreaming tends to happen spontaneously and it is generally prompted by how unreal your dream is. You will recognize something isn't right and that is what creates the instant lucidity. It could be something as silly as the sun being blue or a talking animal. No matter the circumstance, you'll notice that it's not quite right and that is where DILD begins.

DILD dreams happen more frequently than WILDs. A study of 76 lucid dreamers showed only one-quarter of them were wake initiated. The man who'd completed the study, Dr. Stephen LaBerge, believed even those numbers were skewed. It's his belief that WILDs occur more frequently in a lab setting than they do at home.

There are eight different types of DILDs and we will discuss them briefly.

The first DILD is Cycle Adjustment Technique. (CAT). This was developed by a lucid dreamer in Britain by the name of Daniel Love. This technique is simple and involves adjusting the time you wake up every day. This naturally influences the chemistry in your body which will in turn increase your consciousness during REM sleep.

Dream signs are something that everyone has. Lucid dreamers are able to recognize them more easily. A dream sign is a clue that lets the dreamer know they are in an altered reality. As time goes on and you are able to increase your awareness of dream signs, you'll find it easier to have spontaneous lucidity in dreams.

Meditation and dream incubation are two techniques that aid in lucid dreaming. Easy breathing and guided meditation tips can be found online and mastering those will help improve lucid dreaming. Meditation aids in visualization and self-awareness, which will lead to your ability to incubate your desired dream themes.

The fourth type of DILD is Mnemonic Induction of Lucid Dreams. For all intents and purposes, we will use the acronym MILD. This is a method created by Dr. LaBerge and it combines several of the individual DILD skills we are outlining here. MILD involves dream recall or journaling, reality checks, visualization and affirmations, which are self-hypnosis.

Next are reality checks. Performing one of these while awake means you are questioning your conscious experience even though you know you are awake. Reality checks in the dream world are an entirely different experience and provides a different type of revelation.

Self-hypnosis provides a myriad of application in terms of personal development. Self-hypnosis is usually attained through meditation and affirmation. This form of technique is quite a challenging technique and will require a lot of practice.

Subliminal Induction of Lucid Dreams (SILD) affect your conscious perception. Subliminal inductions are images that flash by too quickly for the waking brain to comprehend them. However, the subconscious is great at catching these.

The last subgroup for DILDs is Wake Back to Bed, which is another sleep cycle adjustment. With WBTB, you will create a period of wakefulness early in the morning, before going back to bed. This will improve dream recall and promotes greater consciousness within your dreams.

You can use one or any variation of all eight methods listed above to help spring yourself into DILDs. As mentioned at the beginning of the chapter, DILDs tend to happen naturally. These steps arc simply something to be used to help get you into lucid dreaming.

Chapter 9 – Controlling Your Dreams

One of the most crucial parts of lucid dreaming is learning to control them. Not only is it crucial, it is a really fun part of dreaming with lucidity. There are no limits. You can teach yourself to do anything you'd like in your dreams, which is what gives you control. Certain techniques are designed to give you that control and in this chapter, we are going to look at a few of the most popular themes in lucid dreaming. Ultimately, you are in control of your dream. These are just a few ideas to get you started. As you practice, you'll find what works best for you.

The first most common dream is that of flying. It's highly likely we've all experienced this dream in the past, but we had no control. To be able to manipulate a flying dream is truly an exhilarating experience. It's important to note that flying dreams aren't always easy to control. It's not something we can do in real life, outside of an airplane of course, which makes it hard for the conscious brain to comprehend. Don't worry. That's what practice is for.

First, start out small, tell yourself that you are jumping up and down by visualizing it. (telling yourself the story is very useful also) Then start Hopping or skipping down the dreamscape with small bounds, gradually increasing in distance and height as you go along. You will need to allow your dream body to feel lighter and lighter with each jump, with both visualization and self-explanations of the image of you going higher and higher until you become weightless. Keep in mind that while you are dreaming, you cannot get hurt. Don't let fear limit you. With enough practice, you'll be flying with eagles in no time. Along the lines of flying, you can also try riding on the back of a Pegasus, using a jet pack, or even having giant wings of your own.

Another common theme in lucid dreaming is changing the scenery or the dreamscape, in which we will go through very shortly in more detail. Like flying, this isn't something that is easy to accomplish on the first try. It takes practice. Watching the landscape of your dream change right before your eyes is also moderately difficult. Luckily for us, researchers of dream lucidity have come up with ways to change the landscape in a conscious dream.

Traveling through time is a common and awesome theme. It is one of the simplest ways to learn to control your dreams and to have the experience of time travel. It doesn't necessarily involve flying, but if you are able to master that, it'll make time travel simpler. All you need to do is fly above the clouds; so high you are unable to see the ground below. Visualize the time you want to be in and as you descend, keep that era in the forefront of your mind. Once you get to the ground, you'll be exactly where you want to be! Another option is to use a time machine. Press buttons, pull levers, enter the date you wish to travel to just like Marty McFly in *Back to the Future.* Do whatever you need to convince yourself you are actually in a time machine. The great thing about these methods is they can also work to change the landscape in your dream.

Another theme is to find dream objects. Thanks to dream research, there are dozens of ways to find objects in your dream. It is unlikely for an object to materialize right before your eyes and the key to this theme is visualization. Just like changing the landscape in your dream, if you visualize the object you wish to find, it is highly likely to be there when you turn around. In finding objects, you can improvise as you go along. Visualize the object in your pocket, a drawer, box, or behind a tree. The possibilities are endless.

Talking to your unconscious is simple enough when you've learned to lucid dream. You will be able to speak directly to your unconscious and gain a deeper understanding of yourself and your perception of the world. Once you've become lucid, the best way to have a conversation with your unconscious is to make it real. Imagine another you or an animal that you'd like to talk to. After they are directly in front of you, ask questions you'd like answered.

Knowing how to control your dreams is a great way to achieve feats you might not be able to in your waking life. You can do anything in your dreams. Your goal in lucid dreaming is to decipher the signs and find new and exciting ways to control your dreams.

Chapter 10 – The Scenery is Bliss

There is a significant number of ways to change the scenery in ones' dream. But every dreamer has their own unique way of doing so. I am now giving you an insight into several of the most popular and effective techniques in order to achieve your goals. I myself have used these and they have certainly been successful, although I found the door method to work best.

Firstly, **the door method:** This specific technique is useful for not only changing scenery but also for teleportation. Whilst you are moving around your dream and you wish to change scenery/ places completely, you go through a door and imagine a new place on the other side as you open it, if you are in an established area this is easier. If the area you are in is not established such as an open grass field you will need to stand up and either tell yourself or imagine a door behind you and as you turn in a 180-degree circle it will appear directly behind you.

Secondly, **using time:** If you are wanting to change not only the scenery but also the season or year that you are currently in, then you need to look at a form of clock whether it be that stunning watch on your wrist or simply a clock on the wall. Gaze your eyes upon the time for 10 seconds minimum and as you're watching the seconds tick by imagine the arrow spinning faster and faster until you find its just whirling away time. Once you have watched the time fly by for approximately 20 seconds you will find all of the surrounds are blurry, then you just imagine a time and place where you want to be when you stop and shift focus away from the time.

Thirdly, **pure imagination:** Imagination within lucid dreaming is a main key. To be able to control your imaginations will allow you to implement this method. If you are in a dream where you are in the middle of a busy street and all you want is to lay on your back in a field full of fresh flowers under the sun, imagine yourself there. It takes a little bit of brainpower. You probably won't see it appear before your eyes, but when you turn around, the field will be there. As you walk into it, the scene behind you will change from the bustling city to the field and you will be surrounded by beautiful, peaceful landscape. The most important thing to remember with changing the scenery in a dream is you have to honestly believe that the landscape will change with your thoughts. In order to change the scenery some people can actually close their eyes and imagine the scene they want to be. then when they open them, they are expecting that scene to be there. Others may find that it's helpful to describe the scenery they want to change in words, with their eyes closed which can make the imagination work in more detail. A draw back to this particular method is that it **makes the dream unstable** or causes them to wake up. Hopefully this will not be the case for you and you have a strong hold of your dream. Using the mediation methods later in the book will help you to strengthen your mind control.

Last but not least, **flip the Switch:** If you are looking to change the time from night to day, then this will be helpful. In order to implement this, you will need to imagine a switch wherever you are and just be able to flick it on or off and imagine that it has gone dramatically one way too far then retracts back to a visible state. For example, if you wish to turn a light off and create darkness, you flip the switch and imagine it going pitch black. Then as you adjust your eyes back slowly into focus make it to be dark but still have some sense of sight. The same goes for if you want to turn your dream from night time to day time. Flip that switch and imagine you have hit an extremely bright white light then dim it back to normal daylight. (turning around once you have hit the switch may help for some).

If you believe in star signs and things of this calibre studies show that dreams featuring very bright lights mean that you will solve a problem by learning to look at it in a new and different way. It is a sign that you should trust your instincts more often than what you do. To lucidly dream of switching on lights foretells an unexpected reward for a past kindness. To switch out lights suggests that you will have a holiday or a well-earned rest from your everyday life.

Although according to study's a dream of red lamps is a warning of danger due to uncontrolled passion or temper towards someone or something. If you are to dream of flickering or flashing lights this suggests that someone or something is preventing you from solving a current relationship or family problem. It could be your own preconceptions or emotions that are getting in the way of doing so.

Chapter 11 – Sexually Charged Lucid Dreams

As we've discussed, lucid dreaming is learning how to control all aspects of your dreams, including those wonderful sexual fantasies we all have, but few of us talk about. In our dreams, we can do as we please and when it comes to sexual lucid dreams, the same rules apply.

You might be wondering if lucid dream sex is even possible. The answer to that question is, absolutely! It is a little more difficult to initiate sex in a dream, mainly because your brain has a much different agenda while it sleeps. Because figures and people in your dreams are unconscious projections of your personal psyche, their mission in your dream is probably not to have sexual relations with you.

Ultimately, it is possible to have lucid dreaming sex if you are able to discover what motivates the person in your dream. Instead of trying to immediately initiate sex, try having a conversation with them first, just like a first date only this is happening in your dream. As a matter of fact, it is good for you to try and cultivate healthy friendships and relationships with the figures in your dreams. Be warned that if you are abusive to the figures in your dreams, what you thought might be a good, sexual, lucid dream might turn into a lucid nightmare.

You might also be questioning whether or not achieving an orgasm in a lucid dream is possible. If teaching yourself to fly is a possibility, so is having an orgasm in your dream. As a matter of fact, there is scientific research to support this. Scientists have discovered that lucid dreams can elicit a real, physical response including an increased heart rate, muscular reactions below the belt, and even changes in vascular tissues.

Likewise, this can be purely in the mind, but that doesn't make it any less real to the dreamer in their intensely real lucid dreaming environment.

Because lucid dreaming isn't something most people can launch right into, the same applies to having a sexually charged lucid dream. Like we've discussed in previous chapters, the key to having lucid dreams in general is to hold onto your conscious lucidity right up until that critical point. It's much better to learn all the ins and outs of controlling your dreams and making them lucid before you try to get into sexually charged lucid dreams.

Eventually, when you are ready, this can be achieved by following the steps we've already outlined in this book. Hold onto your consciousness as you slip into the dream world. Once there, set your intention. If you want to find Brad Pitt or Scarlett Johansen (or whomever you are most attracted to), make that your intention and set out to achieve it. Throughout your dream, remember to remind yourself that you are dreaming. And, don't forget to treat your dream man or woman well. Talk to them first and see where the dream conversation takes you.

Chapter 12 – Knowing You're Dreaming

One of the main elements of moving from a normal dream into a lucid dream is knowing that you are in a dream state. During sleep, the conscious mind shuts itself down to allow for rest and your unconscious takes over. Most of the time when we sleep and are having a particularly interesting dream, or nightmare, we don't know that we are dreaming until we've woken up. Once awake, you clearly realize what happened was a dream. If you can realize that while you sleep, you will be able to have lucid dreams and begin to control them.

There are several steps to helping you realize you are in a dream. The first may seem counterintuitive, but once we detail it, you'll understand.

Step one is to check whether or not you are dreaming while you are still *awake*. Sounds silly, right? Trust me, it is a crucial step. Lucid dream researchers and advocates say that doing this during your waking life will help form a habit while you sleep. If you are consistently asking yourself, "is this a dream?" while awake, it'll roll over into your sleep habit. Some things you can try are reading a piece of paper, checking the time and trying to move objects. Obviously, those things would work while you were awake. In a dream, if you fail to do any one of those, you'd recognize you were dreaming. Doesn't seem so silly now, right?

The next step (keep in mind these do not need to go in any particular order) is to perform a reality check. We covered this briefly during the WILDs chapter and will detail it a little more here. These are also things that can be done during your waking life to form that habit whilst you dream. Reality checks, inspect your surroundings and see if everything around you is fuzzy or hazy or are the surroundings crystal clear? Even lucid dreams have that soft focus element to them. While you are awake, everything would be what is considered *normal*. You can feel the carpet beneath your feet, if you pinched or scratched yourself, you would be able to feel that as well. Remember that things are far different in a dream, lucid dreams included. Perhaps your dog is walking backward or the clock you got in the habit of checking during your waking life is spinning out of control. Those reality checks during your waking life will help you to realize when you are dreaming as well.

Check your environment. In the dream world, appearances are often deceiving and distorted. If your dream is occurring at home or work or any place you spend a lot of time, check to see if anything is out of place by looking at common objects. Is the table where it should be? Are the doors and windows lined up as they are in your waking life? Is there a painting where a window once was? These are all easy things to spot in your dream if you look hard enough and are able to focus properly.

Take into consideration the people around you. If you are having conversations with people who have been dead for years (a common theme not to be concerned with), then clearly you are dreaming. Why you are having a conversation with them is an entirely different dream theme, but the fact that they are there is a sign you are dreaming. Other common themes surrounding people are having friendly conversations or even drinks with people you are not friends with in your waking life. Are the people around you complete strangers? If so, you are dreaming. If your grandmother is exhibiting signs of having a superpower, that is also a dream.

Look at yourself! Are your hands and feet correctly proportioned? Do you have the right number of fingers and toes? Is your hair its normal color and length? Take a look in a mirror. In a dream state, you don't usually look like yourself. The reflection looking back at you will be blurry or even distorted.

There are several ways to test yourself to see whether or not you are dreaming. These are just a few. Once you've determined that you are, in fact, dreaming, the next phase is to test your limits.

Chapter 13 – So, you're dreaming...Now what?

Testing your limits is a great way to leap into lucid dreaming. Earlier in the book, we talked about common lucid dream themes. Now, we want to see just what you can do in this dream state. Testing strength and ability is one of the first things you'll want to do once you realize you are dreaming. Try moving something heavy. It should be something you wouldn't be able to move on your own while awake. A large television, a bed or even a boulder depending on where you are in the dream.

Start teaching yourself to levitate or float. Like flying, this is something that takes practice. Always remember that in dreams, there are no limits. Do something you've always wanted to in your waking life, but limitations kept you from achieving it. Explore what it would be like to have god's strength. You can start out small with levitation but once you realize the sky is the limit, there is literally nothing you can't do.

Another neat thing to try in your dream is supernatural abilities. Move something with your mind, manipulate the elements in the world around you by making it rain or snow, make objects appear from out of nowhere. Use your imagination and make your dreams the place you can explore free of the limitations you experience while in your waking body.

You've officially moved from recognizing you are in a dream and now it's time to manipulate it. Research shows that keeping a dream journal while you are starting to explore the world of lucid dreaming is a great tool to come back to. If you've kept a journal, go back and read some of the things you experienced prior to trying lucid dreaming. In dream land, you can bring some of those awesome dreams back to life and accomplish the things you weren't able to before.

While you explore the things you can do in your dream, maintaining control is key. Depending on your personality, you might enjoy some chaos or enjoying being able to make your sexual fantasies come true from time to time. For the most part though, once you've stepped into the world of lucid dreaming, you'll want to maintain that control by staying focused and lucid at all times.

Without mental focus, things will begin to waver in terms of your levels of consciousness. Your dreaming self will consistently try to take over and add its own elements of dream imagery. Ultimately, you'll end up in a battle between your conscious self ego and your dream. In order to maintain control, there are three key elements you'll want to keep in mind. Remember, lucidity is the ability to maintain a certain level of conscious awareness in the dream state. That means setting up some expectations before you go to sleep.

First, make sure you cement your lucidity once you've achieved it. There are a few tricks to cementing lucidity and as you practice, you'll find what works best for you. Some people like to rub their hands together as if they are preparing for something great. Consciously taking a deep breath and exhaling audibly is another way you can cement the lucidity. As always, reminding yourself that it is a dream is the best and easiest way to cement things.

Along the lines of telling yourself that you are having a dream, you'll want to consistently remind yourself of that throughout your dream. Lucidity can fade if you aren't using this trick at regular intervals and once the dream evolves on its own, you've lost control and there usually isn't any going back.

Finally, set a lucid dream intention. Your intention can be whatever you like. Perhaps before you went to bed you decided you wanted to try to fly or travel through time. Once you've entered the lucid dream, remind yourself of your intention and seek to complete it.

These three simple actions, which take only a few seconds to implement in your dream world, will cement your intentions and keep you on track throughout your dream. It will be incredibly frustrating for you to lose that control. Remember though, this will happen from time to time and it is all a learning experience. There is no reason to be angry with yourself, learn from it and try again the next night.

Chapter 14 – Meditate Your Way to Lucid Dreams

The art of meditation offers more benefits than getting into lucid dreaming. It is good for your overall health to take a few moments every day (longer if you can) to appreciate your body and give it some quality time to itself. You can do this through yoga, meditative breathing and guided meditation. Those are only a few ways to meditate, but are a great way to get yourself one step closer to lucid dreaming. And, let's face it. You do a lot in your daily life. Not only does meditation give you some time to relax your mind and body, it gives you some peace and quiet. Who doesn't want that?

Meditation is part of the WILD technique we discussed previously. It also goes hand in hand with MILD, another form from earlier in this book. Meditation can aid in improving your in-dream skills such as visualization and focused states of awareness, which is where your lucid dreams will become longer.

There is scientific research to back this up. These studies show direct links between meditation and lucid dreaming. They both involve using a higher state of awareness, help you become more focused, reflective and self-aware. Meditation also helps to improve your dream recall, which is key in lucid dreaming.

Let's talk a little bit about what exactly meditation is. The art of meditation has been in practice for at least five-thousand years. Almost every religion employs some form of meditation. However, you do *not* need to be religious to meditate. Meditation itself stems from psychophysiology. This is a branch of psychology that studies how the mind can affect the body. To meditate your way to lucid dreaming, you'll need to develop two skills, which are quite contrary and opposite to one other. Those skills are; **focus,** which is a higher degree of mental concentration. The second skill is **quicscence,** which is finding that quiet, stillness in the mind.

What's great about meditation is you don't have to sacrifice your social schedule or family time to meditate. There are two simple routines we will outline here which are breathing to calm the mind and guided meditation to find your focus. Really, both are quite enjoyable and are a great way to escape from the daily routine in your life. Even if it is briefly.

The first form of mediation is simply breathing. Our bodies naturally breathe in and out so that we can live. Finding the right breaths while meditating is different, yet simple.

Find a quiet place. This kind of meditation requires you being able to sit with your back straight. You can sit on the floor with your legs crossed or in a chair. The straight back is important so that you don't meditate yourself to sleep.

Close your eyes and start to focus on your breaths' in through your nose and out through your nose. At first, you won't want to try to control it. Just take note of the pattern. Is your breath rapid, shallow, deep? Be aware of how air enters and exits your body and how it feels as it goes through the motions.

When you first get into your meditative position, you'll find your mind might be racing and your thoughts jumbled. That's okay. It's why you are taking the time to meditate. If it feels like your mind is getting busier, that's also okay and completely normal. It means you are heightening your sense of self-awareness and are beginning to notice just how many thoughts you actually have. Impressive, isn't it? Make sure to avoid following any of those trains of thought as it would be a distraction. Continue to focus on your breath as it goes in and out of your nose.

If at any point you realize your mind has wandered, bring yourself back to your center and focus on your breathing. It can take ten to fifteen minutes for you to achieve that quiet state of mind you are seeking. Once you get there, your thoughts, while still active and in the forefront of your mind, will become lucid and clear. Remain in this state for as long as you feel comfortable. Again, if you've only a short period of time, that's okay. Try to practice this form of meditation every day. You can do it before you go to bed at night, or first thing in the morning. Those are likely the easiest as the hustle and bustle of life can make it difficult to take a seat and meditate in the middle of your day. That being said, you might find great benefit from taking a time-out during your day to meditate. Keep in mind that this breathing technique is also great for combatting anxiety. Slow, deep breaths fight off the rush of adrenaline from stress.

The next form is known as guided meditation. This is where you will focus your mind. Once again, you'll find a quiet place to sit down remembering to sit with a straight back to avoid falling asleep. Guided meditation is where you will increase your self-awareness and in your mind, you will disassociate yourself from your physical form.

Guided meditation is where you can use your imagination. Picture yourself walking through a beautiful, wide open meadow. The sun is shining; the flowers are in bloom. It is peaceful and serene. Feel that fresh air fill your lungs and then exhale slowly. Take a moment to fully appreciate and observe your surroundings.

The point of this technique is to use your ability to visualize to increase your awareness of your imaginary landscape. During this process, you'll be letting go of all your everyday thoughts and anxieties. Listen intently to that blissful silence. You might even be able to hear birds singing, the sound of thunder and perhaps raindrops as they hit the ground. The stronger you can get this mental imagery, the better off you'll be.

As you start to go deeper into your meditation, feel the grass beneath your feet. Stop and smell the red roses, feel their soft petals, take note of the warm air as the breeze gently brushes over your skin. All of your movements in this state should be slow and deliberate. Here, you can take as long as you'd like and truly enjoy the beauty around you. If you find that it helps you to keep moving instead of stopping regularly, that's okay too. This is your practice. You do what feels best and what helps you maximize your meditation. Moving might make the scenery change, and that's also okay. Just make sure you notice it as you continue on your path. Take note of the scene as it changes. Remember, this is a key element in self-awareness for lucid dreaming.

Like breathing meditation, guided can take in upwards of fifteen to twenty minutes to get into the deep, trance-like state. Once there, you'll have little awareness of your physical body and it might feel like you are on an entirely different plane of existence, which is a freeing and wonderful feeling! You can remain in this state for as long as you'd like. There are no limits. The only thing you need to remember is that you must get to that trance-like state before ending your meditation. Otherwise, it won't be a true, guided meditation. When you are there, try to stick around for a few. This is about you and taking the time your body needs to get a break from itself.

After you've been in your guided meditative state for a reasonable amount of time, you'll want to *gently* rouse yourself from this state. Don't startle yourself out of it. Take deep breaths and count backward from ten. Perhaps take one slow, deep breath for a count of ten, then your exhale is nine, so on and so forth. After you've come out of the meditative state, take another moment or two before you open your eyes. It will give your body the opportunity it needs to acclimate to being back to reality.

These two completely self-guided exercises will help you increase your self-awareness. They allow your mind to focus without any distraction. Make it unique to you and take the liberty of changing the scenery from time to time to keep things fresh and exciting. You can go so far as to make up your own, out of this world scenes. What's important is to make sure they are relaxing. You wouldn't get much out of meditation if your scene involves inter-galactic space battles taking place around you. You'll want to promote vivid mental imagery while maintaining that calm relaxation.

There is one final note to be made on the topic of meditation. There are several meditation aids you can use if you find it difficult to concentrate. In the way of free sounds, you can use Pandora. However, if you have the free version, know that even their meditation station is prone to commercial interruption, which might be counteractive to what you are trying to achieve. You can also download one of several meditation apps to your smartphone. Some are free and have no commercials while others cost up to two bucks. Finally, there is a new product out called Muse. It is a meditation headset that can make meditation easier. The brain sensing headband is designed to provide real time feedback as to what is going on inside your brain. This is pricey, however and costs around two-hundred and fifty dollars.

Conclusion

Thank you again for taking the time to download and purchase this book!

You should now have a good understanding of Lucid dreaming, and be able to not only determine when you are dreaming but have the skills to control your dreams.

Happy dreaming to all of those that took the time and effort to practice the techniques you have now learnt.

If you enjoyed this book, follow on to the sequel 'Advanced Lucid Dreaming' in a few months when it is released. Please take the time to leave me a review on Amazon. I appreciate your honest feedback, and it really helps me to continue producing high quality books.

3 1502 00827 5453

Made in the USA
Charleston, SC
15 December 2016